Ubuntu 16.04

Easy guide for beginners

Table of Contents

Introduction

Ubuntu is one of the various Linux distributions. It is well known for its ease of use especially by Linux beginners. It comes in both desktop and server versions. The desktop version is the best one for beginners due to its ease of use. It provides the users with a graphical user interface which makes it easy for them to navigate through the system. With Ubuntu, it is easy for one to install software applications and even find hardware which is connected to the system. This book is an excellent for you on how to use Ubuntu 16.04. Enjoy reading!

Chapter 1- Getting Started

Ubuntu is one of the user-friendly Linux distributions. It is easy for one to setup and begin to use it. To download Ubuntu 16.04, open **http://www.ubuntu.com** then head to the Downloads section. Once you are done with downloading Ubuntu 16.04, install it.

The system should be updated daily or weekly. First, refresh the repositories:

sudo apt-get update

Next, run system updates:

sudo apt-get upgrade
sudo apt-get dist-upgrade

Your system will be updated.

Customize the Ubuntu System

With Ubuntu 16.04, it is possible for you to choose where you need to display your menu. The menu can be displayed on the app windows or in the top bar. The various menu items can also be disabled from auto-hiding.

To exercise control over the menus, open System Settings, then Appearance, then go to Behavior tab. From there, you can control the visibility of your menu.

The Desktop

The Ubuntu 16.04 desktop has a number of similarities to the desktops of other operating systems. The concept of GUI (Graphical User Interface) is supported in these operating systems. You can use the mouse to open applications, navigate the desktop, move files and do many other tasks. The Ubuntu desktop helps in presenting tools to the users visually. Let us discuss the various tools and elements of the Ubuntu desktop:

Desktop Background

This is the image which covers the whole desktop. It is the default desktop background or wallpaper for Ubuntu 16.04. It belongs to Ambiance, which is an Ubuntu 16.04 theme. However, this can be changed.

Desktop Customization

To customize the desktop, one should open the Session Indicator, and then choose System Settings. This will launch the application window for System Settings. From this window, you are able to access the Dash, themes, wallpapers, desktop appearance, accessibility and many other settings.

The Look tab

From this tab, one can change the window theme, background and the size of the Launcher icon, and then have a new look and feel of the desktop.

Right click on the desktop then select "Change Desktop Background". You can also choose "Session Indicator", then "System Settings", then "Appearance". Choose "Look" tab.

The "Appearance" window will show the theme and wallpaper which are being used currently. To change the Background, you can choose Wallpapers, Colors and Gradients, or Pictures Folder from the drop-down list. Click on *Wallpapers* and you will see the default selection of backgrounds by Ubuntu. You can click the picture you need to use as the background and you will see it change. If you need to use your own picture, just click the + button then navigate through the system to the image itself. Click *Open* and you will see the change take effect immediately. If you choose the *Pictures Folder*, all pictures will be opened and you will be able to choose one for your background. The button for *Colors and Gradient* will allow you to change the background to solid or gradient color. If you need to use a solid color, click the button for *Solid Color*, then *Pick a Color*.

It is also possible for you to change the size of the icons on the launcher. Use the slider provided below Look tab, and then chooses a range between 32 to 64 pixels.

Behavior tab

This tab has numerous options which can be used for changing the behavior of the desktop:

• Auto-hide the Launcher- this will help you show the launcher whenever you move the pointer to a defined hotspot.

• Enable workspaces- this option will help you enable workspaces when turned on.

• Add show desktop icon to the launcher- this will help you show the desktop icon on launcher when it is turned on.

• Show the menus for a window- this option can help you show menus in window's title bar or in the menu bar.

• *Menus visibility - there are two options for changing how visible a menu is. In the first option,* the display will be done once the mouse hovers over application window. With the second option, the application menus will always be displayed.

Screen Reader (Orca)

This is a good tool for people who experience difficulties with vision. Ubuntu 16.04 comes with this tool pre-installed, and it provides the readers with "Screen Reader" functionality in a Universal Access.

To activate it, use any of the following ways:

1. Via keyboard shortcut by hitting ALT-Super-s keys.

2. Clicking Dash to open Orca.

3. Navigating through Session Indicator -> System Settings... -> Universal Access -> Screen Reader -> ON/OFF.

Logging out

Once you are done with your task, you may choose to log out, restart, suspend or shut down your computer. This can be done via Session Indicator, which can be found on far right side of top panel. When you log out, the computer will be left running, but you will be taken to login screen. It is a good idea when you need to switch users, or maybe log into the system as a different user.
You can press Ctrl+Alt+Del so as to log out of the system. Ensure you close all open applications and you have saved your work before logging out.

Suspending

When suspended, you will save energy and your current open applications will be saved in the RAM, and starting again will be quick. To put the system in suspend mode, open the "Session Indicator" then choose "Suspend".

Rebooting

Open the "Session Indicator", chooses "Shut Down..." then click Restart icon. The computer will reboot.

Shutting Down

Shutting down the system will power it off completely. Open the "Session Indicator", chooses "Shut Down..." then click Shut Down icon.

Other than the above options, the Session Indicator has other options. You can choose "Lock/Switch Account..." to switch the user accounts or to lock the current user's screen. This is good if you will be away from the computer for an amount of time.

Getting Help

Ubuntu comes with Ubuntu Desktop Guide from which you can get help. To access this, click the Dash then type "help".
 You can also access it by pressing the F1 key while you are on the desktop, then from menu bar's Help menu, choose "Ubuntu Help".

However, if you don't find an answer to your problem, get online help by posting your question on **http://ubuntuforums.org**.

The Menu Bar

The menu bar has a number of components very useful in Ubuntu. There are many icons on the right side of the menu, and this area is called the *notification area* or *indicator area*. The following the available indicators:

1. Network indicator- this icon can help you to connect and disconnect easily to both wired and wireless networks.

2. Test entry settings- show the current layout of the keyboard, which can be Fr, En, and Ku etc. It also provides you with a way to choose the keyboard layout. The menu for keyboard indicator has items such as Character Map, Text Entry Settings and Keyboard Layout Chart.

3. Messaging Indicator- for incorporating social applications. It allows you to access email clients and instant messenger.

4. Sound indicator- with this, you can get a way to adjust the volume of your sound system and access sound settings and music player.

5. Clock- this shows the current time while providing a link heading to the calendar as well as time and date settings.

6. Session indicator- this provides a link to the system settings.

The Launcher

This is the vertical with numerous applications icons and found on the left side of the desktop. It provides the user with a quick way to access the Trash, applications and mounted devices. As an application runs, its icon is placed on the launcher.

If you need to change the size of launcher icon, navigate through Session Indicator -> System Settings ->Appearance, tab Look.

At the top of the launcher, we have the Dash as its first icon, and this is a component of Unity. Other applications which can be found in the launcher include the LibreOffice, Files file manager, Firefox and any mounted devices. You can hold the Windows key (Win key), also referred to as the Super Key, which can be found between Alt key and the left Ctrl key, will cause the system to add a number to the first 10 applications on this launcher. A screen will also be displayed showing a number of useful shortcuts. This number can be used to launch an application when you press Super+n, where n is the number assigned to the application.

Sometimes, you may open many applications than the launcher can show. These will be folded, so you only have to point the mouse to the bottom of the launcher and more applications will be shown.

For you to start an application, you only have to identify its icon on the launcher then click it.
The following are the various ways of adding applications to the launcher:

1. Open the Dash, look for the application you need to add to launcher, and then drag its icon to launcher.

2. Open the application to be added it, right click its icon on the launcher then choose "Lock to Launcher".

If you need to unlock an application from the launcher, right click its icon then choose "Unlock from Launcher".

This Dash

This provides you with a way to search for applications within the system. Through the Dash, you are able to search for the installed applications as well as the remote applications such as Google Docs, Twitter etc.

To access it, click its icon on the launcher, which is the top most icon with Ubuntu logo on it. You will then see a search bar, and the desktop will be covered by some translucent window.

Lenses

These are used in the Dash for searching. For one to search, they must use one or more lenses, and each lens provides its own category of search results in the dash. Six lenses come installed by default, including Home lens, Application lens, Video lens, Files and Folders lens, Photos lens, Music lens.

For you to search for a file, application or folder, you just have to type half of its name in the search section of the dash. You may be provided with numerous search results, so you will have to choose the right one.

Other than searching for the applications installed on the computer from the Dash, you can search for various online resources from the Dash. This option comes disabled by default. To enable this option, navigate through System Settings -> Security &Privacy -> Search then turn on the "Include online search results" option.

Workspaces

These are also referred to as virtual desktops. They help one to group applications, reduce cluttering on the desktop and provide an easy way of navigation. Example, you can open your office suite in one workspace, media applications in some other workspace, then a web browser in another workspace.

This feature is disabled by default. To activate it, navigate through Session Indicator -> System Settings -> Appearance and click the Behavior tab then click the box for "Enable Workspaces". Once enabled, you will see another icon added to the launcher.

For you to switch from one workspace to another, you must click the workspace switcher icon on the launcher. You will then choose the one that you need.

If you need to move a particular window to another workspace, you should first ensure that it is not maximized.
If the window has been maximized, just click the right-most button located on left side of title bar in order to restore it to original size. You can then right click the title bar of the window then choose:

• Move to Workspace Left in order to shift the window to left workspace.

• Move to Workspace Right to shift the window to right workspace.

• Move to Workspace Down to shift window to bottom workspace.

• Move to Another Workspace in order to choose the workspace to which you need to move the window.

Keyboard Shortcuts

If you need to view all the available shortcuts, just long press the Win key, which is also known as the Super Key?

Browsing for Files

For you to browse to a file, you can search for it or access it directly from its directory. To search for a file, you can use the Files file manager or the Dash. These two can also be used when one needs to access the mostly used directories and files.

The Home Directory

This is the directory where all your personal files are stored.

Note that other users who have accounts with the PCF can access the contents of your home directory. The home directory is created during the creation of the account and it must match your login username. During installation of Ubuntu, several directories are created including the Desktop, Documents, Public, Music, Pictures, Videos, Templates etc. However, it is possible for you to create as many directories as you need.

The Files File Manager

To open the Files file manager, choose the Files shortcut on the launcher, click on the directory in Dash, or just double click any directory on the desktop. You will get the default window with a number of features including Desktop, Documents, Videos, etc. These can help you access the files you have stored in any of those directories.

Creating Directories

You may need to create some new directory from within the area for the Files file manager. To do this, move to the right pane then right click the blank area and a popup will appear. Choose "New Folder". The folder will be given a default title, which is "Untitled Folder". Just replace this with the name of your choice. Instead of going through the above steps, you can simply press Ctrl+Shift+N so as to create a new directory.

Hiding Files and Directories

For you to hide a particular file or directory, you just have to place a dot (.) at the beginning of its name. If you have named the folder "My Documents", then change this name ".
My Documents" so as to hide it. For you to view the hidden files, simply press "Ctrl+H" or just click View, then choose "Show Hidden Files". However, note that using a dot to hide some files and directories is not a security practice, but it provides one with an easy way to organize their files.

Playing around with Files and Directories

From the Files file manager window, you can play around with files by copying, pasting and even cutting them. You only have to right click the respective file within the window. A pop up will appear, and you will be able to choose the option that you desire. Also, you can achieve this by pressing keyboard keys such as Ctrl+X, Ctrl+V and Ctrl+C to cut, paste and copy files respectively within the window. If you need to choose multiple files or directories, left-click on an empty space, hold down the mouse button then drag your cursor across the files and directories that you need to choose. This is a good way of choosing items which have been grouped together.

Chapter 2- Software Applications

For you to accomplish your tasks on Ubuntu, you should have software applications installed. Let us discuss some of the software applications.

Office Suits

There are various office suits in Ubuntu. LibreOffice is the most popular office suite in Ubuntu. It includes the following:

- Writer- a word processor
- Draw- a drawing program
- Impress-a presentation manager
- Base- a database
- Calc-a spreadsheet
- Math-an equation editor

By default, the LibreOffice comes pre-installed in Ubuntu. However, by default, Base is not installed, so you must install it via the Ubuntu Software Center. You may also try other office applications such as Gnome Office, KOffice, Gnumeric (a spreadsheet application), Kexi 9 a database application) and many others.

Email Applications

There are numerous options for you when choosing the email application to use in Ubuntu. The popular one is the Mozilla Thunderbird. This can also be used on Windows. Note that Ubuntu provides Thunderbird as the default email application. You can also choose to use KMail or Evolution.

PDF Readers

Ubuntu provides Evince as the default PDF reader. There are also alternatives such as Adobe Reader and Okular.

Web Browsers

Firefox is used as the default web browser in Ubuntu. If you don't like, try its alternatives such as Epiphany, Chromium, Opera*, Midori and Google Chrome*.

Podcatchers and Music Players

There are various applications which can be used in Ubuntu to listen to music. Rhythmbox is the most popular one and it comes installed by default. Others include Audacity which can be used as a sound editor, Amarok, VLC, Micro which can also play videos and others. With these applications, you can listen to your podcasts and music. Micro is the best application if you are in need of watching TV shows and podcasts from the internet. With VLC, you will be able to play various music and videos of different file formats.

Photo Applications

For you to view and manage your photos, you can use Shotwell which is the default application for photo management in Ubuntu. You can also use applications such as Gwenview, gThumb, F-Sport and others.

CD/DVD Burning Applications

In Ubuntu, there are several applications which you can use so as to burn applications to DVDs. Examples include Gnome-baker, SimpleBurn, Brasero, Xfurn, cd burner and K3b. Most of these tools provide the users with a user-friendly interface, making it easy for you to use them.

Graphics Editing Tools

You can use a tool named GIMP to edit your graphic applications in Ubuntu. With this tool, you can modify your pictures, taper your photographs and even create own graphics. You can also use Inkscape, which is a good tool for creating and editing Scalable Vector Graphics images. These two tools are not pre-installed in Ubuntu, but you can install them via the Ubuntu Software center.

VoIP Applications

With VoIP (Voice over IP) applications, you are able to talk to people over the internet. Ubuntu comes installed with Skype, which is a very popular application for such communications. You can also use Ekiga, which is an open-source VoIP application which works using SIP protocol. Skype is incompatible due to the fact that it uses a proprietary protocol.

Instant Messaging Applications

Some of the most popular instant messaging applications in Ubuntu include Pidgin, Kopete and Empathy. These tools communicate over common protocols such as aim, msn, irc, Jabber/xmpp, Google Talk, Yahoo, Facebook and ICQ.
You will only need one application so as to be able to communicate with your friends. However, a number of these applications have a limited support for videos.

BitTorrent Clients

Ubuntu provides us with numerous BitTorrent clients. Transmission is used as the default one, and it is light-weight and easy for anyone to use. Others include Vuze, Deluge and KTorrent which come with numerous features which can help in supporting the advanced users.

Chapter 3- Internet Connections

For you to access the internet with Ubuntu, you can use a dialup connection, a wired or a wireless connection. There are also several advanced options for one to connect to the internet with Ubuntu.

For the case of a wireless connection, your computer uses a wireless radio network so as to connect to the internet, which is commonly referred to as a WIFI. Majority of modern routers now support wireless capabilities similar to laptops and desktop devices. This type of connection is very popular due to its portability.

For the case of a wired connection, the computer uses an Ethernet cable so as to connect to the network. The cable is normally connected to a socket plugged on a wall or to a networking device such as a switch or a router.

For the case of a dialup connection, the computer uses a model so as to establish a connection to the internet.

The Network Manager utility is used for management of network connections in Ubuntu. With this utility, you can manage both wired and wireless connections, turn the network connections either on or off and create network connections such as VPNs, dialup and mobile broadband.

The Network Manager icon is provided in the top panel, so use it to access the utility. Once you click the icon, you will see all the network connections which are available. Any connection with an option for "Disconnect" underneath will be connected. You can click this option so as to disconnect your computer from this. You can also edit your current connection details from there.

If you need to disable all the network connections, you only have to deselect the option for "Enable Networking". If you need to enable this, you will have to select the option for "Enable Networking". This is a good way for you to turn on and off the network connections.

Connecting to a Wired Connections

It is possible for you to be actively connected to the internet. This is because the connection might have run successfully during the setup process for Ubuntu. You can launch your browser and search for something to check whether you are connected to the internet.

However, you may not have established a wired connection to the internet. You may have an Ethernet cable running from a networking device such as a router or switch, or from a wall socket.

Before connecting to a wired connection, first determine whether the network is capable of supporting Domain Host Configuration Protocol (DHCP). It provides a way for computers to automatically access the internet. The DHCP is configured automatically on the router. It provides one with an easy way to connect to the internet. If the router doesn't support DHCP, then you should know the necessary configuration settings for you to access the internet. This calls for you to contact your ISP or LAN network administrator.

If the network supports DHCP, you are ready to connect to the internet. Click the Network Manager icon. You will see a heading for "Ethernet Network" in the menu. If you see either "Auto Ethernet" or "Wired Connection 1", your machine will be readily connected to the internet, and readily configured to use DHCP. If you see the "Disconnected" option underneath, look below for the "Wired Connection 1" option. Click it and establish a connection.

If this fails, you may have to use a static IP address to configure the network. Let u discuss this:

Manual Configuration

For the case of networks which do not support DHCP, you must know a number of details so as to be able to establish a connection. These include an IP address, a network mask, a DNS server, a gateway, and the network mask.

For you to connect manually to a wired network connection, first click the network icon then choose "Edit Connections". If you identify any connection listed like "Wired Connection 1", just click it then choose "Edit". If you don't see any connection, click "Add" button.

For you to add a connection, you must give it a name. This will distinguish it from any future connections. In the field for "Connection Name", type a name for the connection.

The connection can then be setup as follows:

1. Ensure the "Connect Automatically" option, which can be found below the connection name, has been selected.

2. Open the "IPV4 Settings" tab.

3. Change "Method" to "Manual".

4. Click "Add" button located next to empty list of addresses.

5. Type the IP address in the field below "Address" header.

6. Click the right of IP addresses, then type the network mask. If you don't know it, use 255.255.255.0 as it's the common one.

7. Click the right of network mask then type the address of the gateway.

8. In the field for "DNS Servers", type the address of the DNS server. If you are adding more than one, then use a comma to separate them.

9. Click "Save" in order to apply the changes.

The new connection should then be listed in the screen for Network Connections. Click "Close" so as to return to the desktop.

Connecting to Wireless Network

If your computer has a WIFI network adapter and you have a WIFI network in your area, you need to be able to use it from your Ubuntu system. The Ubuntu OS is capable of detecting the available network connections in your area. For you to view all available network connections, begin by clicking the Network Manager icon. All the available network connections should be listed below the "Wireless Networks" option.
Each will be identified by its name and the relative signal strength. Identify the WIFI network you need to connect to then click its name. If the network is not protected, the connection will be established quickly without being prompted to enter a password. If the connection is successful, the signal meter will be displayed showing the strength of the signal. You will also see an on-screen message telling you that the connection has been established.

If the network has been protected with a password, the Ubuntu will display the "Wi-Fi Network Authentication Required", where you will be required to enter the network password. Just type the right password then click "Connect". If you need to see the characters you type for the password, click the checkbox for "Show Password".

If the connection is successful, you will see the signal meter showing the strength of the WIFI signal. An onscreen message will also be displayed showing the connection has been established.

Once you have connected to a network, whether wired or wireless, Ubuntu will always connect to it once detected. However, many networks may have been saved, and the system may connect to a network you don't want. To solve this, click the Network Manager icon. You will see a list of all the available network connections. Click the one you need to connect to, and you will be disconnected from the previous network.

Connecting to Hidden Network

Some wireless networks are hidden, meaning that they do not broadcast their names.
Their names cannot be seen in the list of the available network connections. For you to be able to connect to such a network, you must get its name and other security details from the ISP or network administrator. You can then follow the steps given below so as to connect to it:

1. On the top panel, click the Network Manager icon.

2. Choose "Connect to a hidden wireless network". A new window will be opened.

3. In the field for "Network name", type the name of the network. This is the service set identifier (SSID). The name should be typed in the same way it is while including any special characters used in the name.

4. Choose an option from the field for "Wireless security". If you are connecting to "Open" network, leave it to "None".

5. Click "Connect". If the network is password-protected, you will be asked to type a password. If correct, a connection will

be established, and an onscreen notification will be shown telling you that the connection has been established.

Connection Mobile Broadband Network

In case you have a mobile device capable of supporting tethering, then you can connect to it from your Ubuntu system. Such devices include Android mobile phones and tablets. You must enable tethering on the device. This varies from device to device. After that, connect the device to your computer, most probably through a USB cable and it will be shown in the list of available connections which can be accessed from the Network Manager icon.
 Note that after the connection, your traffic will be send through the mobile network of the carrier provider and data rates may be applied.

Once you are connected to the internet, you can launch a web browser such as firefox and browse the internet.

Chapter 4- Ubuntu Software Center

The Ubuntu software center provides Ubuntu users with an easy way to install software applications. It is also an easy way to find any software applications that you may be in need of. You can get access to thousands of applications through the Ubuntu software center. Some of the applications can be downloaded for free but others are commercial. Each application which can be found through the Ubuntu software center comes with ratings, so you can choose the best one to install based on these ratings.

To launch it, open the dash then search for "Ubuntu Software", or just click its icon from the launcher. The applications installable from the Ubuntu software center are the ones provided in the official Ubuntu repository. The window for Ubuntu software center is divided into four sections including Featured Application, Recommended Applications, Editor's Picks and Categories. Once you click any category, you will be shown a list of related applications.

To open its main page, click the "All" button. To see all the applications already installed, click the "Installed" button. To see any available updates, click the "Updates" button. If you need to search for the application that you need, just type its name in the search bar. The search bar can be found in the top panel of the Ubuntu software center window. If you don't know the name of the application you are looking for, you can click its category, for example, Audio category. Browse through the list of provided applications then choose the right one.

Software Installation

After finding the application that you need on the Ubuntu Software center, you can install it. The following steps can help you install the software:

1. Click on "Install" button.

2. You will be prompted to enter a password in the authentication window. This should the password for the account.

3. Once the password is accepted, the installation of the software will begin. Wait for the installation to complete. After that, an icon for the application will be added to the launcher.

You will then be able to use the application. You can launch it by opening the Dash then searching for its name.

Uninstalling Software

To uninstall an installed application, open the software center and search for it. You can also click the Installed button and you will a list of all the installed applications. Look for the application that you need to uninstall, and then click the "Remove" button. You will be asked to verify whether you are sure you need to remove the application. You will be provided with two options, Remove and Cancel. Click on Remove in order to continue with the uninstallation process. You will be prompted to enter your password, so do those? The software will be uninstalled, and the menus will be updated accordingly.

Additional Software Repositories

The Ubuntu software center will only show you the applications which are available in the enabled repositories. It is possible for you to add other repositories, or download and install software manually. The Software & Updates application can help you to add extra repositories.

To open the Software & Updates, open the "System Settings" then click "Software & Updates" from the System section.

After opening the Software & Updates, you will be able to see Ubuntu Software tab, and this comes with the first four options enabled. These include the following:

1. Canonical-supported free and open-source software (main)

This repository has all open-source packages being maintained by Canonical.

2. Community-maintained free and open-source software (universe)

This repository has all open-source packages which are developed and maintained by Ubuntu community.

3. Proprietary drivers for devices (restricted)

This repository has all the proprietary drivers which many be needed for one to use all the features of some devices and hardware.

4. Software restricted by copyright or legal issues (multiverse)

This repository has all the software which is protected for use in some countries or states by licensing and corporate laws. Note that once you use this repository, you will take responsibility for any software that you may install and use.

5. Source code

This is a repository with the source code needed to build software packages from other repositories. You should select "Source code" option only if you have experience in development of applications.

Adding Software Repositories

With Ubuntu, it is easy for you to get third-party sources of software applications. PPAs are the popular repositories to be added to Ubuntu. It stands for Personal Package Archive. They are simply online repositories where latest versions of software applications are stored. With them, you are able to install software applications which are not available in official repositories. With PPAs, you can get automatic notifications whenever there are available updates.

If you are aware of the web address of the Launchpad site for your PPA, you can add it to list of software sources. This can be done through "Other Software" tab which can be found in "Software & Updates" window.

On the PPA's Launchpad site, you will see a head named "Adding this PPA to your system" on the left side. Below this, you will find a small paragraph with a unique URL. Select this URL, right click it then choose Copy.

Open the Software & Updates window then in the tab for "Other Software", click "Add". You will see a new window with a section for "Apt line:" and a text field. Paste the URL you copied in the text field by right clicking it then choosing Paste. Click on "Add Source" so as to go back to Software & Updates window. You will see that a new source will have been added.

Installing Software Manually

You may be in need of software which is not available in the Ubuntu repository. This calls for you to install it manually if it does not have any PPA. However, be sure that you trust the package as well as its maintainer.

Ubuntu packages normally have a .deb extension. Once you double click a package, you will be taken to its overview page and you will be able to view more information regarding the package. Once you click "Install", the software package will be installed.

Ubuntu Updates

In the window for Software & Updates, the "Updates" tab will allow you to manage the package updates. You can decide the kind of updates that you will want to be installed in the system.

At the middle part of the window, you will be allowed to customize how updates are treated in your system, such as the frequency with which the system looks for the updates. You are also able to choose whether the system downloads the updates found, installs them or just notifies you.

While in the Updates tab, you will see the "Notify me of a new Ubuntu version:" option at the bottom. This section helps you instruct Ubuntu on how it should treat the release updates. It has the options given below:

1. Never- with this option, you'll never be notified about Ubuntu releases.

2. For any new version- choose this option in case you need to always get the latest Ubuntu release. It is the best option for the normal home users.

3. For long-term support versions- this is the best option for those who need a more stable release and one which will provide you with support for longer time.

Chapter 5- User and Group Management

After a new installation of Ubuntu, only a single user can use it. If the Ubuntu system is to be used by more than users, then it is good for each user to have his own account. With this, each user will have his files, settings and documents. With this, you are also in a position to manage the users able to view your files by restricting access to your files to users with certain permissions only.

Other than using different accounts, Ubuntu supports the use of groups through which you can assign permissions to different users at once. Every user in an Ubuntu system belongs to at least one group. All users of a particular group will have same permissions. It is possible for you to configure files and folders to only be accessed by certain users and groups. By default, only the owner of a file can access the file and only the root user can access the system files.

User Management

If you are using an administrator account, you can use Users and Groups administration application so as to manage the users and groups. To access the application, navigate through Session Indicator -> System Settings... -> User Accounts, then click "Unlock" button. You will be asked to enter your password, so do so in order to unlock user settings. Next, choose a user you need to modify. Next, click on the element that you are in need of modifying.

Adding Users

To add a new user, click the + button located below the list of the available user accounts. You will see a new window with three fields. The field for "Account Type" will show you the list of all the user account types. You must be keen to assign each user the right type of account. The *Standard* account type will have a limited access to the resources of the Ubuntu system, while the *Administrator* account type will have full access to all the parts of the Ubuntu system. The field for "Full Name" will have a friendly display name. The field for Username represents the actual name of the user. Once all the necessary fields have been filled, click the "Add" button. The newly created user will then be added to the list of the available user accounts.

By default, new user accounts are disabled, so you must enabled them. To enable the account, just click the field for "Account disabled" located next to "Password" label. You will see a new window which will ask you to set a password for the new user.

You will also see a dropdown menu on the new window next to the label for Action. The option for "set a password now" will be selected by default. You can also choose "log in without a password", but note that the account will be made available to everyone. The option for "enable this account" will be made available once the password for the account has been set. With this option, the administrator will be in a position to enable or disable the account without losing the password.

Group Management

In Ubuntu, groups are only managed via the command line. However, you can still add third-party applications and you will be able to manage groups.

To add a new group, you should first launch the command line by pressing Ctrl+Alt+T. You can also search for "terminal" from the Dash, and then click it when presented. To add a new group, run the following command:

sudo addgroup groupname

The "groupname" should be replaced with the name of the group you need to create. Once done, hit the enter key. If you need to create a group named "students", you will run the following command:

sudo addgroup students

For you to add a user to a group, use the command given below:

sudo adduser username groupname

The "*username*" should be replaced with the name of the user to be added to the group, whole the "*groupname*" should be replaced with the name of the group to which you need to add the user. After typing the command, hit the enter key to execute it.

If you need to delete the group, execute the following command:

sudo delgroup groupname

The *groupname* should be replaced with the name of the group that you need to replace.

Sometimes, you may need to change the group that a particular file or folder belongs to. To do this, just launch the Files file manager then navigate to that file or folder. Right click the file or folder then choose "Properties", or select menu Files, then Properties. On the dialog window for Properties, click "Permissions" tab then choose the group you desire from Groups dropdown list. You can then close the window.

Chapter 6- Basic Security Features

It is good for you to keep your files secure. Ubuntu comes with a number of features which can help in the implementation of security. Let us discuss these:

Permissions

Ubuntu allows one to control how files and folders are accessed, viewed, modified and executed by use of permissions. You may need to grant some users access to certain files, but you may not need them to alter the files. In Ubuntu, such control can be exercised using permissions. The permissions are simply settings which can be configured in order to control how the files on the computer are accessed and used. Permissions can be set using the chmod (change mode) command from the Ubuntu terminal. "r" represents a read permission, "w" represents a write permission while "x" represents an execute permission. To add a permission on a file or folder, use the + (addition) operator and to remove a permission from a file or folder, use the − (subtraction) operator.

Passwords

It is always good for you to use a password so as to ensure your system remains secure. Avoid using common words, names and phrases as passwords. This is because one can easily guess them and log into your system successfully. By default, Ubuntu allows a minimum of 4 characters to be used as the password. It will be good and safe if you use a password which is longer than this. It is recommended that you combine numbers, symbols and both lowercase and uppercase letters when creating a password for your Ubuntu system.
Screen Lock

When your computer is not in use, you may need to lock the screen. When locked, no user will be able to access the computer unless they enter the right password. The following steps can help you lock the screen:

From the top right corner of top panel, identify the session menu icon then click it. Choose "Lock/Switch Account..."

Or:

Press Ctrl+Alt+L keys in order to lock the screen. If you need to change the keyboard shortcut, navigate through "Session Indicator-> System Settings... -> Keyboard -> Shortcuts" then choose "System" from the left column, then click "Lock Screen" option provided in the right column.

Chapter 7- Adding a Printer

Ubuntu is capable of supporting a wide variety of hardware. Each new release of Ubuntu comes with an improved support for new hardware. Ubuntu also provides you with numerous ways which you can use in order to identify different kind of hardware. The best way for you to do this is by installing an application known as *Sysinfo* from the Ubuntu Software center.

Just open the Ubuntu Software application, search for sysinfo then click the "Install" button. When prompted to enter your password, just do so and the installation process will continue. To use the application, just open the Dash then search for "sysinfo". Click it once found and you will see its window showing all the hardware in your system.

You can connect your printer to your Ubuntu system. For you to add, change or remove printer properties, you can navigate through "System Settings", then "Printers". You can also open the Dash then search for "Printers". You will see the window for "Printers-localhost".

When adding a printer, make sure that it is switched on. The printer should be connected to the computer either via a network or by use of a USB cable.

If the computer has been connected to the PC using a USB cable, then it is known as a local printer, while a printer connected to the PC via the network is known as network printer.

To add a local printer, ensure it is switched on and connect to the PC via a USB cable, then click "Add Printer". In the pane on the left hand side, click the printer that you need to install then click the "Forward" button. You will then be able to specify the name of the printer, a description and its location. Once done, click "Apply".

For you to connect a network printer, ensure that you have connected the printer to the network via wireless network or using an Ethernet cable. Also, make sure that the printer has been switched on. To add the printer, open Printers then click the "Add" button. You will see the window for "New Printer". Click the small triangle next to "Network Printer".

If the printer is found, you will see its name below "Network Printer". Click its name the click the "Forward" button. Specify the name of the printer, give it a description then specify its location. Click "Apply" button.

Also, it is possible for you to add a printer by use of its IP address. Just choose "Find Network Printer" then type its IP address in the "Host" text field, then click "Find" button. The Ubuntu will find your printer then add it. If the printer cannot be found, you will be asked to specify some other details about your printer.

Conclusion

We have come to the end of this guide. Ubuntu 16.04 is easy to use. One can easily understand how to navigate through its graphical user interface. It is also easy for one to change the various settings such as the desktop background and others. The installation of new software in Ubuntu can easily be done by searching for the application you need from the Ubuntu Software Center. The application will be searched from the registered repositories and you will be prompted to install it once found.

Note that you can add several repositories to your Ubuntu system and you will be able to download software applications from them. For you to search the installed applications, especially when you need to use a particular application, you only have to search for it from the Dash. Once found, it will be presented to you and you will only have to click it so as to be opened. With Ubuntu 16.04, you can establish a connection to both wired and wireless network connections. Security is also important for any system.

In Ubuntu, you can use permissions and passwords to ensure that your system is secure. Users can also be grouped into groups. Different permissions can then be assigned to different groups which is good for security of the system.

ISBN 9781981450985

9 781981 450985

90000